DON'T BE AFRAID

by: MaryCynthiaGrace M. Johnsen

Illustrated by: Sandi S. Desai

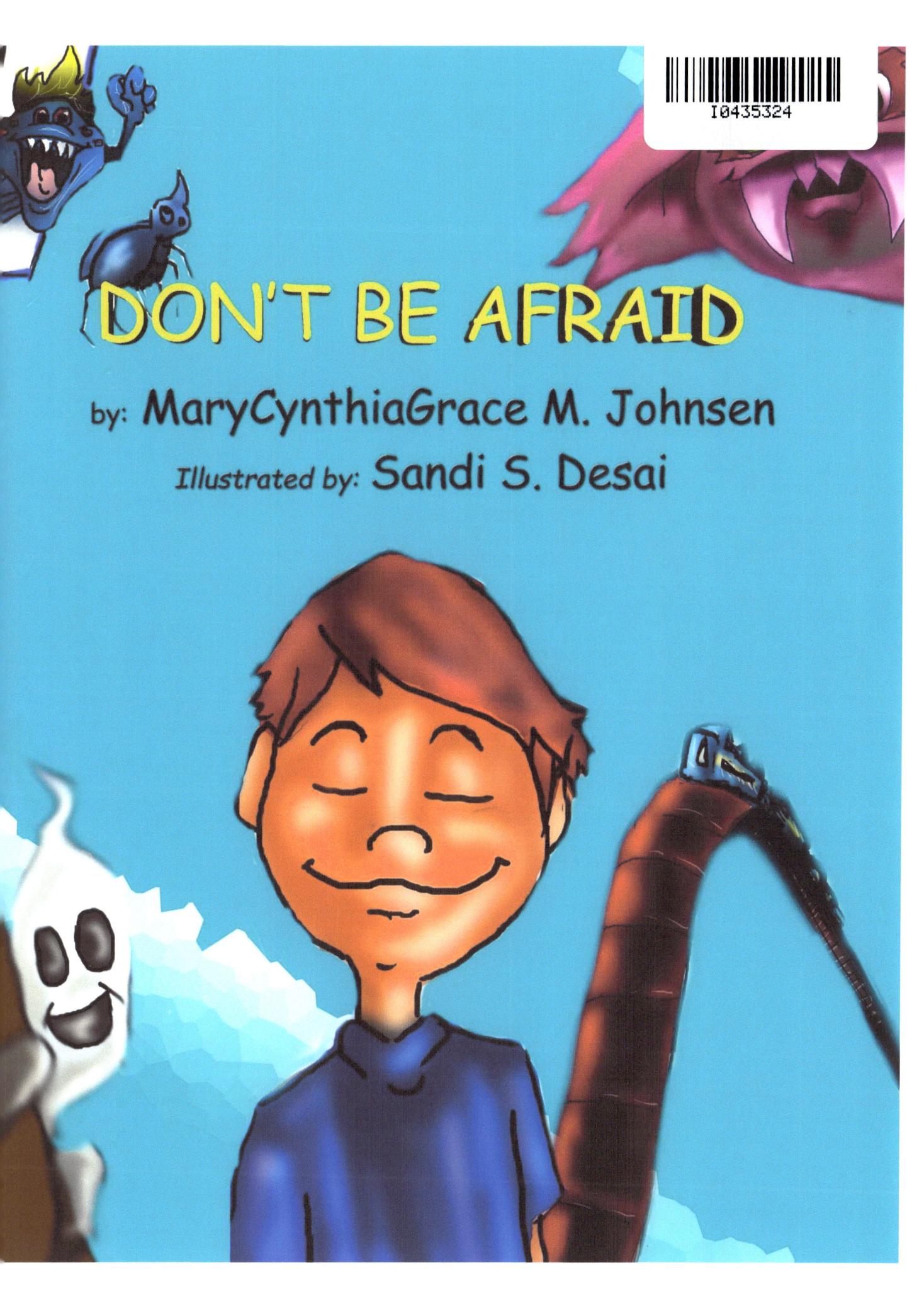

This book is dedicated to

my parents, Oscar and Cynthia, my
loving husband Tim, and my adorable
girls, Hannah and Isabelle.

Special Thanks To

Sandi for being my best friend and
wonderful artist to illustrate this book for
me.

Love you all,
Grace

Dear parents and guardians,

When children feel fear or anxiety they often do not know how to respond. This book was designed to help parents teach their children some calming down techniques. Read this book often with your child and it will soon come naturally.

When reading, pause for a moment after each page to stimulate discussion. The book was designed to prompt your child to reflect on what fear is to them. In the end your children will be able to process their own emotions and boost their emotional management skills.

Enjoy this book!

What makes you afraid?

The Dark?

Roller Coasters?

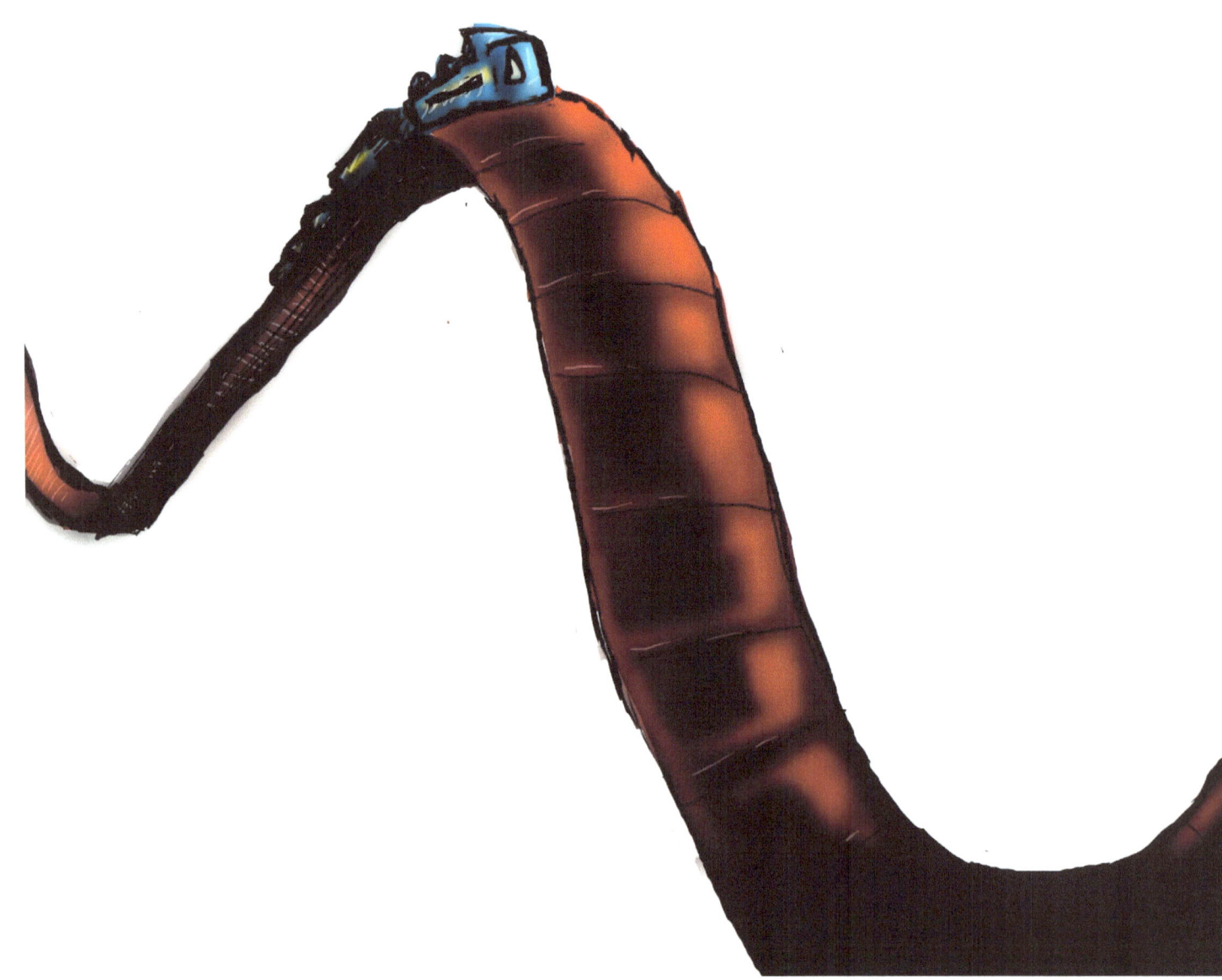

Monsters?

How do you know you are scared?

What happens to your hands when you get scared?

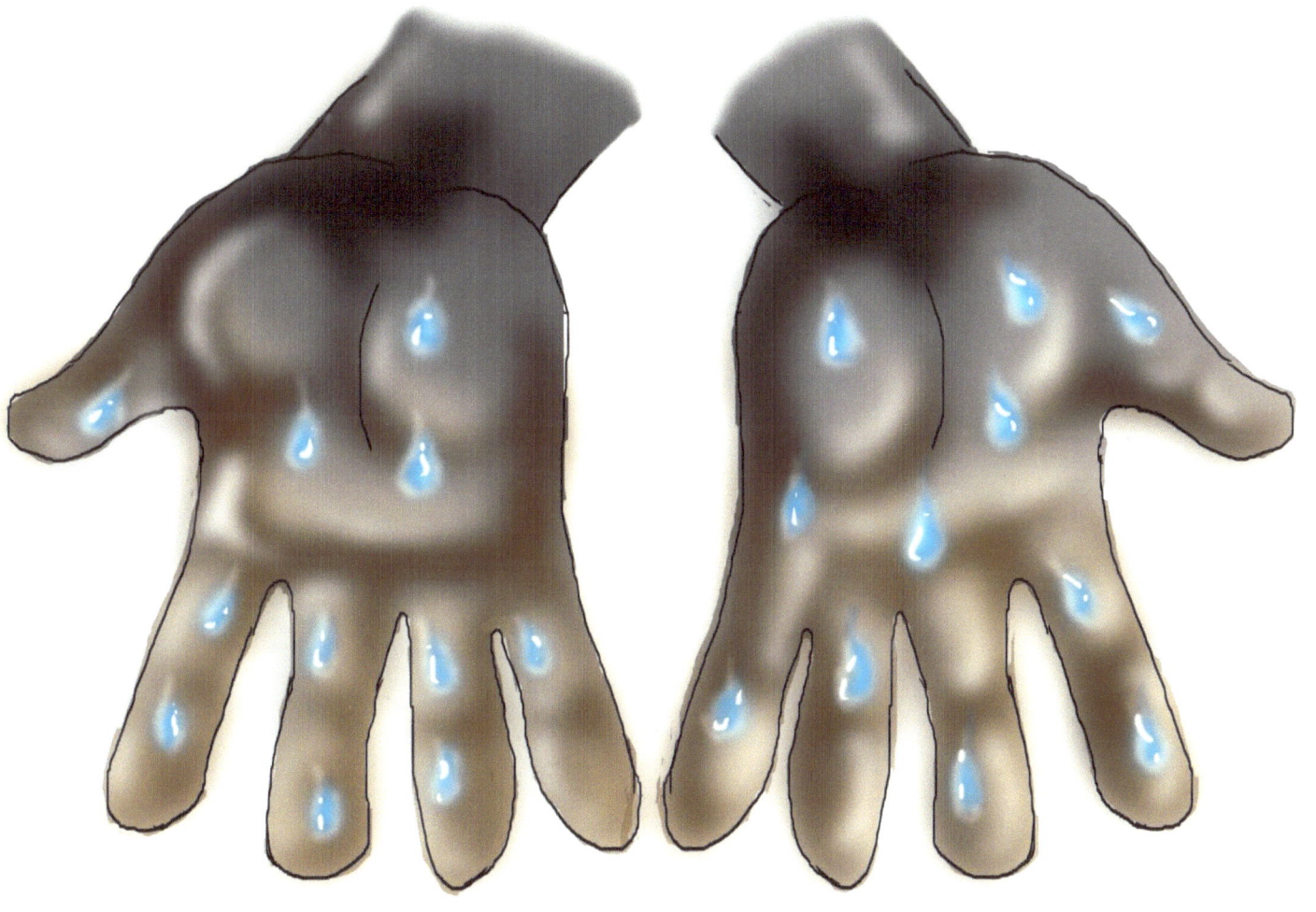

Do your hands get sweaty?

Does your whole body get sweaty?

What do you look like when you are scared?

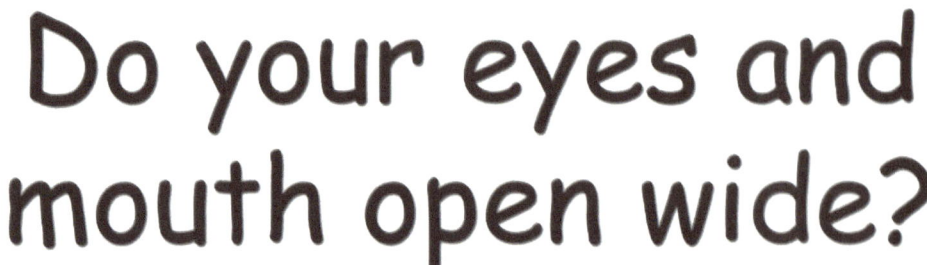

Do your eyes and mouth open wide?

Do you bite your fingers and your nails?

Do you shake or tremble?

Do you breathe heavier and faster?

Does your heart beat faster and louder?

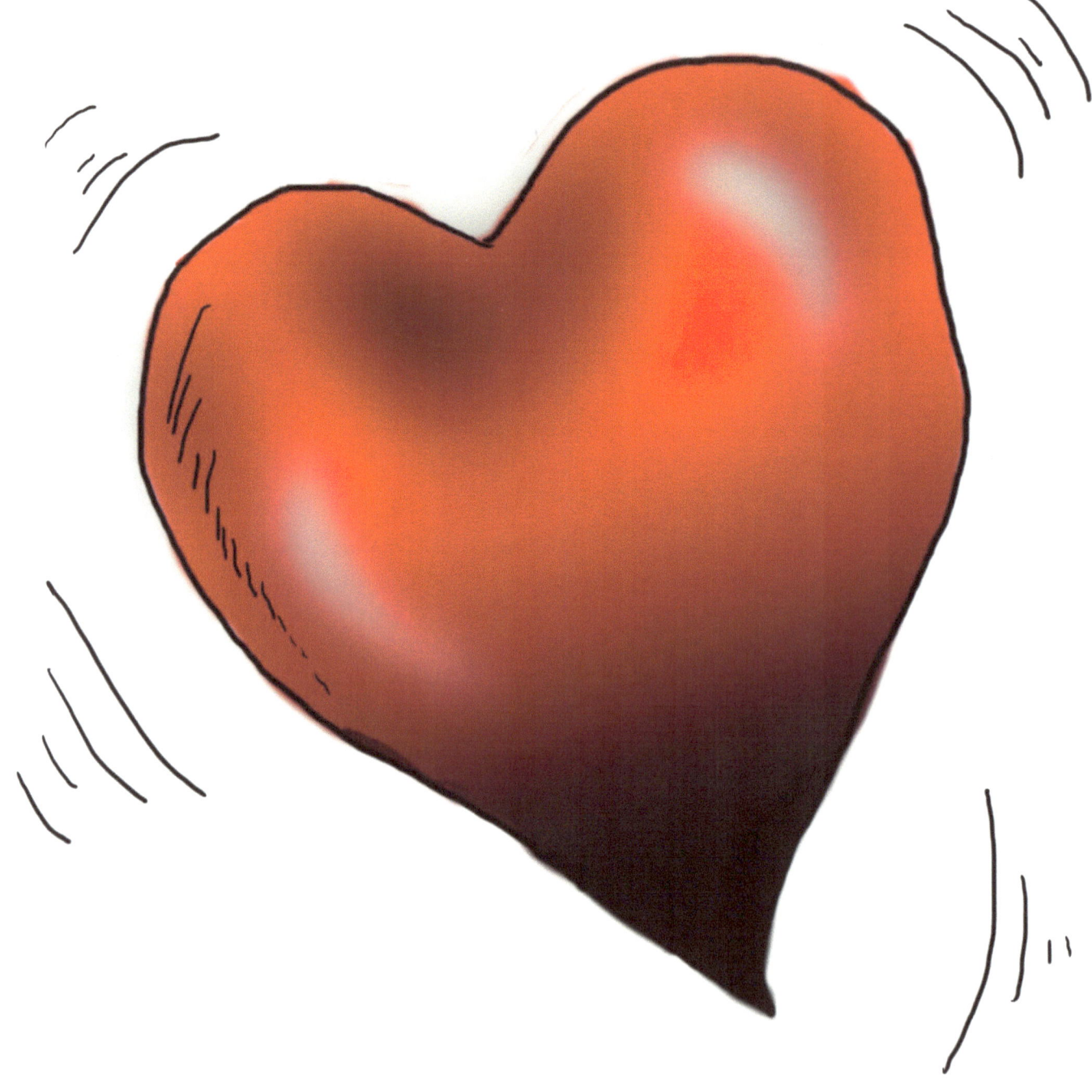

What are you thinking when you are scared?

What do we do when we are too scared to calm down?

Just breathe. Pretend there is a balloon in your tummy. Now breathe in SO much air to make it bigger!

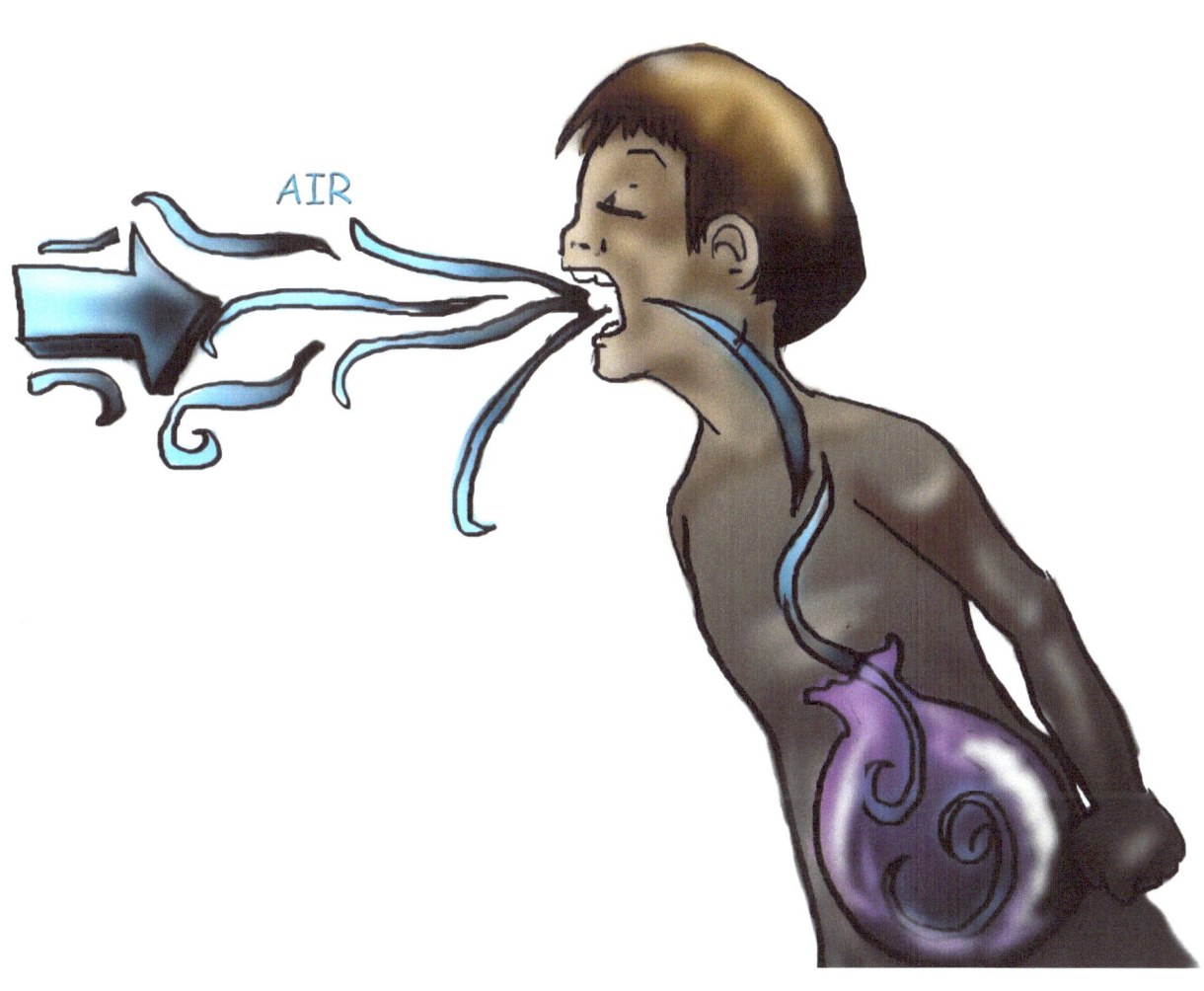

Picture your birthday cake and some candles in front of you.
NOW BLOW!

Then repeat. Breathe in.

Breathe out.

Close your eyes.

See your happy place.

It can be real or pretend.

What do you smell with your nose?

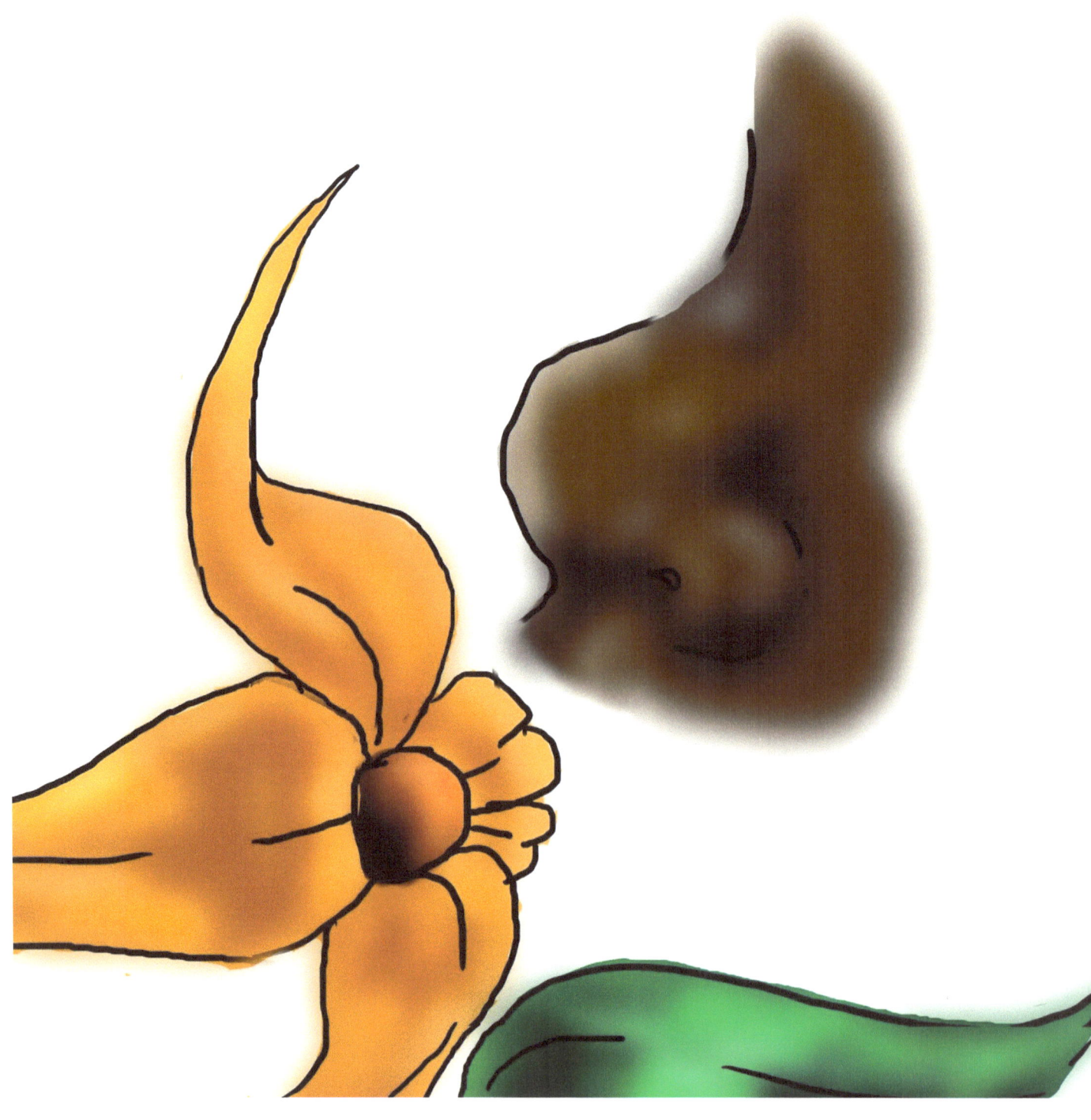

What do you hear with your ears?

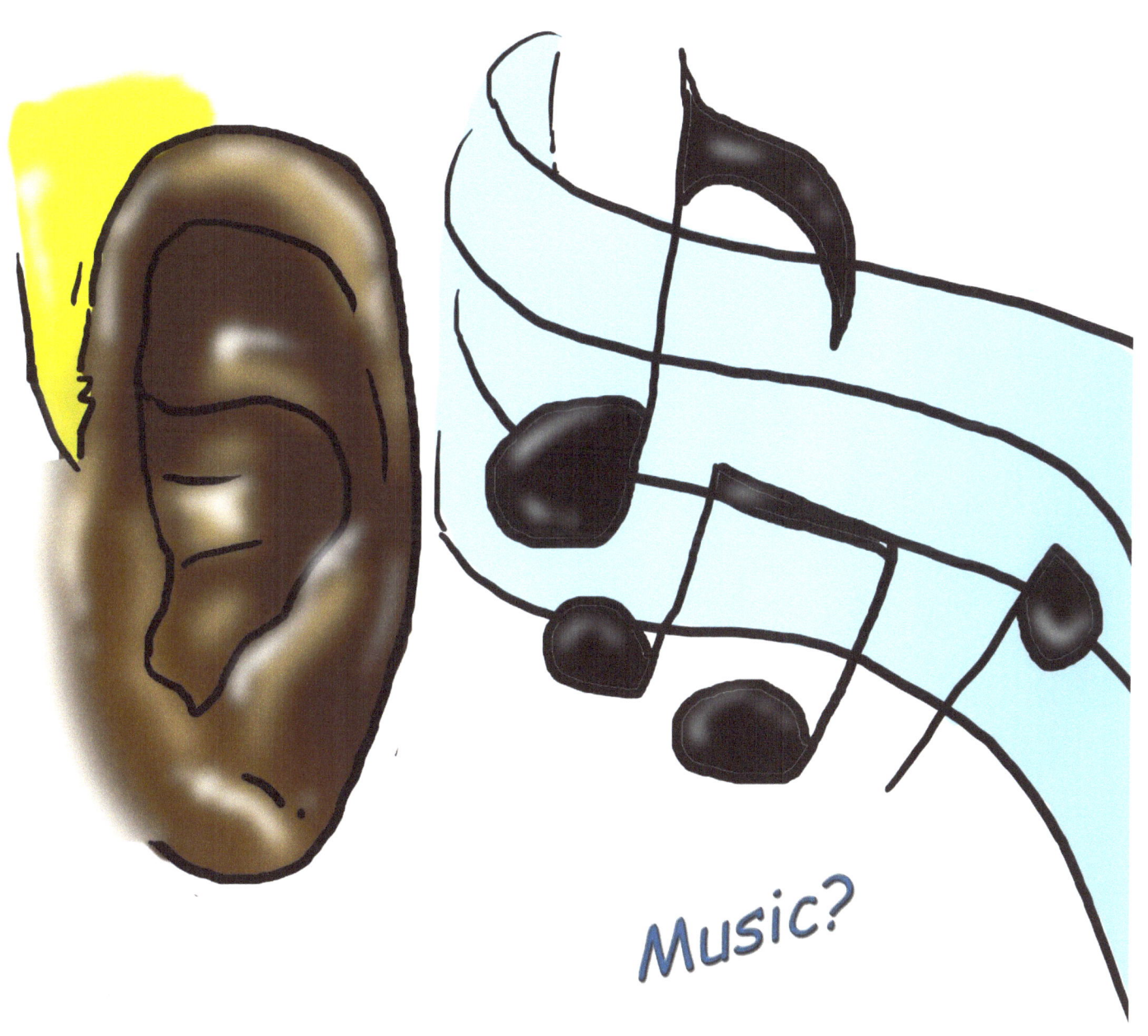

Music?

What can you taste with your tongue?

chocolate?

strawberries?

Is it cold or hot?

Is someone with you?

Or are you alone?

You can open your eyes now.

How do you feel?
Do you still feel afraid?

Practice this until you feel calm.

Written by a mental health counselor and illustrated by a game designer. An eye catching children's book that teaches children how to manage their own fears by implementing *calming down techniques*. This book prompts questions about fear helping parents to enhance their children's communication skills. This is an extremely useful tool for children who suffer from high anxiety.

www.AllThingsByGrace.Etsy.com

HTTPS://WWW.FACEBOOK.COM/MAMAPLAY

American Counseling Association

www.Mystic-SandArt.DeviantArt.com/Gallery